The Heart Map

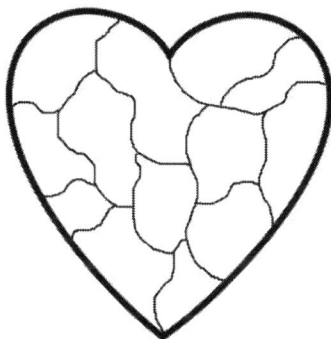

J. S. Brown

THE HEART MAP – J. S. BROWN

Published: February 2021

ISBN: 978-1-7772647-1-0

Instagram: @jsbrown_poetry
Website: https://linktr.ee/jsbrown

For the one that's searching –

You are still someone
While you are out searching for yourself,
While you are out searching
For your purpose.
You will never be a forgotten road.
You are the entire highway;
You are the whole map;
You are the footprints leading you home.

(After Courtney Peppernell)

Table of Contents –

Part One:

Fractures on My Heart

—

"The **fractures on my heart**
Create a map of my past
And future battles."

A Little Broken

Do you feel a little broken?
Is your heart only a mere few beats away
From bursting out of your tired chest?

Do you feel a little vulnerable?
Like a piece of glass – one wrong move
Away from shattering into pieces.

Do you feel a little broken?
Because I do, all the time.

A Letter to Trauma

One day,
I will put my trauma into words.
I will write down what happened.
I will acknowledge it.
I will accept it.
I will make it real.

I don't think it will be easy –
Pulling parts out that I never wanted to see
In the first place but, I will do it.

One day,
I will unzip the trauma from my bag of
Secrets and suffocate it with my words.

I will drag it out of me by its hair.
I will scream.
I will cry.
I will plead for it not to be real.
I will fall to my knees and claw my eyes
Out to escape it but eventually,
I will quiet down.
I will get back up and believe in myself.
My eyes will heal, and I will survive.

Don't Bottle Up Abuse

Writing about you makes me sick –
Like I just drank sour milk, and now
The taste burns on my tongue.
But, how else am I supposed
To deal with the scars
You left on my soul?

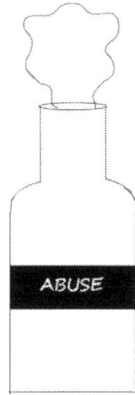

ABUSE

Pretty Deadly

The drugs might keep you skinny,
But how much longer can that
Little frame hold the weight of
A thousand demons?

You've never been happier
With how you look yet,
Tell me, please –
Is it worth having a pretty face
If it's killing you in the process?

The Ghost of You

There's a knot inside my chest,
And it's been there for years.
I thought that I could heal it
Through all these shed tears,
But I realized that it won't go
Because you're still here,
And I just really want
To be rid of this fear.

Vices

We all have vices,
Some more deadly than others.

What makes living so unbearable,
In that we're all forced to search
For ways to cope?

The Attic in My Head

If you're looking for me, I'll be tucked away in the attic. The dust is building up and I'm tired of thinking about you.

I hid all my memories in cardboard boxes, stupid me thought that would be strong enough to keep out the weather. But after years of neglect, the edges are starting to spill my secrets onto the hardwood floor.

So, if you need me I'll be upstairs – cleaning out my brain of all the trauma that I tried to run from, tried to forget.

But my body is not a house – it's my home, forever. And my brain is not an attic, but I can still do my best to keep it tidy when things start to build up.

Words Stain

The walls are stained
With all the nasty things
You've said to me.
And I scrubbed them with bleach,
Until my fingers traced
A crimson map of all the ways
I tried to clean you from my life,
But sometimes when I'm alone
I can still hear them spitting
Vulgar words at me.

Did you ever think that your words
Would leave such permanent stains?

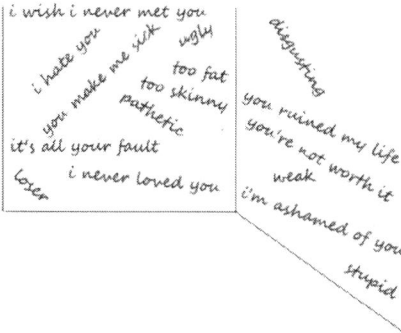

Addict's Fever

I can't shake this fever,
I'm going insane.
My addiction will kill me,
With I to blame.

Swallow the Memory

I know you're holding onto something
That you're just dying to spill.
Every second of the day you're aching to
Scream it out to someone –
Anyone that will listen,
But you've played it over a million
Times in your head already
And it always ends the same: badly.
So, you swallow the memory
For the hundredth time,
And pray that you won't
Recall it tomorrow.

Sandpaper Skin

Your touch felt like
Sandpaper on my skin,
Regardless of how hard
I tried to imagine that your
Fingers were rose petals.

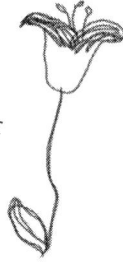

You Never Met the Real Me

I was drunk when we met,
And you hated the person
I was trying to be.

I was high when you called,
And I told you things that
Weren't true.

I was anxious when you held me,
And the trembles in my body
Scared you away.

I was always going through something,
And you always thought that you
Were the one causing it.

But truthfully, you were the only
Thing that was keeping me alive.

Putty-Filled Cracks

There are some things in my life
That I'd prefer to keep
Buried deep down.
But sometimes my walls get weak,
And the trauma seeps its way through
The putty-filled cracks.
So, I must accept that no matter
How many layers of bricks I stack
High in the sky, there's always a
Chance that something terrifying will
Still find its way inside my head.

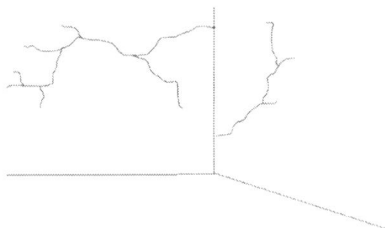

Heavy Memories

And I hope my memory
Never weighs heavy
On your heart.

I only meant to make your wings stronger –
I just wanted you to be able to fly,
But now you're far from being weightless
And it's all my fault.

Scribbles of A Stoner

You could write about the drugs,
But you don't know what to say
Because they've become a part of you.
You could tell me about how
The smoke fills your lungs
And brings you peace –
Leaves you on the edge of ecstasy
For just a second, and then brings you back
Down from the heavens.
You could scream about the times
It made you feel like you could crawl
Out of your own skin.
The times it made you feel
Like you could see someone else
Inside of your own body.
The times it made you question
Even your closest friends.
But, you don't need to talk about
All of that – you don't need to
Go back to that place.
So, I'll believe you when you tell me
That it's your favourite medicine
And simultaneously your darkest curse.

Protect Your Flame

The wind is growing stronger
And your flame is burning out.
You tried to keep the light on inside,
But the dark drove another route.

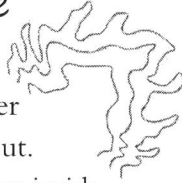

Only You Can Save Yourself

What's pain, when no one can see it – how do you convince someone that your heart is breaking when you're perfectly composed on the outside?

What's hurt, when no one can feel it – how do you explain what's going on when you can't make sense of the war inside your head?

What's love, when not a single person really knows you – how do you trust someone so completely, that you'd let them reach inside and take what you've always protected?

What's death, when you already feel so damn alone – how do you convince yourself to stay, when the whole world is telling you to go?

I'm A Little Volatile

Threats of violence
Turned into threats of action.
And honestly,
I just wish I knew
When I started to let
The rage control me.

Tongue-Tied with Pride

If only I could manage to
Swallow my pride,
Maybe he wouldn't yell
So loud from the back
Of my throat.

Then again,
Maybe he's what I need –
A backbone.
A spine.

But lately, he just seems
To be getting me into trouble.
And boy, do we fight –
We always seem to butt heads.
So, I've found it's best
If I just keep my mouth shut.

Holding Anxiety's Hand

There are so many things
That I'd like to do,
So many plans I've planned.
But when I build
An ounce of courage,
Anxiety takes my hand
To lead me to the lonely prison
That is my own mind.
I've been trapped in there
For so long, just wasting
Precious time.

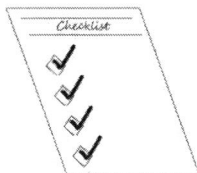

The Revival

I planted peonies
Underneath your ribs,
And wondered why
They wouldn't grow.
Little did I know,
It would take more
Than a few flowers
To breathe life into
Your withered heart.

Betrayal

Perhaps what hurts the most is the idea that the sole you trust the most in the entire world has let you down.

Stop Asking Me How I Feel

I threw up all my feelings for you –
I couldn't keep them down any longer.
You taste like lies
And it makes me sick.

Grant Me Strength

I just want to get it right –
Even for a second,
But it seems as though
When I strive for something,
The universe finds a way
To help me fail.

And I'm thankful for the lessons.
Truly, I will never grow a spine
If I don't test its strength,
But I think I've learned enough
Lessons for this year.

Please, would you just
Grant me some strength
To appreciate my life?
To love myself?

I'm not ready to give in,
To let life take the wheel
And steer me in the wrong direction.
I want to keep pushing,
But I'm so tired
Of getting shoved back.

Black & Grey Rainbows

I'm not a colourful person,
I sure do enjoy the darkness.
From my closet, to my notebook,
And all the way into my brain –
You'll find a rainbow
Of only black and grey.

Alone in A Sea of Billions

I've met so many people
In my short lifetime.
All of which have left
Their own mark on me.

There were those who
Set my heart on fire,
And those who
Left me outside in the rain.

There were abusers who
Turned my heart to stone,
And lovers who
Cracked it open wide.

I've met many different people
In my short twenty years,
Which is why I cannot understand
How I always feel so alone.

Your Sick Friends

I was young and ripe –
Becoming a woman faster
Than my skin could stretch itself.

You paraded hungry boys
Around me, and I obliged –
Thankful to finally be noticed.

But I was much too small-minded
To understand just how wrong it was
For them to objectify me.

Violent Memories

Maybe one day I'll escape
From this room
You've left me to die in.
Right now, I'm far too weak
To even ponder movement.
My eyes have never felt so heavy,
As I watch the life pour from
My veins onto the porcelain floor.
Ruby lay all around me,
And in her warm embrace
I'm convinced that I'll be home soon.
But a violent memory is all it was,
When I awake to find myself
Still locked away within my insanity.

Finish Your Dinner

Sink your teeth into my brain
And chew up all the thoughts of you.
That's how I feel now
When you speak to me –
And there's only so many
Memories left for you to eat.

Trauma Walks Beside You

You could down another bottle
Of whatever makes the pain fade
Or you could learn how to cope
With all the mundane emotions
That you feel.

You feel numb because of
The countless times you've
Refused to deal with the trauma.

I promise you this:
The memories will never fade.
You must learn to be at peace
With the pain they bring
As your trauma walks
Beside you daily.

Swollen Courage

I've been here before –
My heart on the floor.
Courage swollen
And twisted with fear.
I worked so hard to beat this,
So how did I end up here?
Back to where I started,
It always comes to this.
I didn't intend to succumb to
Such eternal pain sealed with a kiss.
But the Devil sits on my shoulders,
Always mocking me with
Eyes that blacken and smolder.
I have so much left to achieve,
So, why do I feel finished?
What will it take for my demons
To be diminished?

Pulling My Thread

You've shown your true colours
And of them, I'm not proud.
Pick apart every inch of me
As you scream your hate, so loud.

My Father says you're no good for me,
But I've never known what he means
When he says that I'm coming undone
And you're the one pulling at the seams.

Bitter Survival

The things one would do just to stay alive…

Lies spun into the tightest webs.
Miles ran until feet bled.
Body parts traded,
And smiles faded.

All for what?
To live with the memory –
The pain of your past.

Being a survivor
Holds immense misery,
From day one to the last.

Passive–Aggressive

I'll tell you that I'm fine with it,
But we both know I'm not.
You stabbed me in the back when
I'm the only ally you've got.

Biting my tongue is easier
Than admitting I'm upset.
Passive-aggressive emotions
Hold nothing but regret.

Crater

Something has been eating
Away at my soul.
With razor-sharp teeth,
It's been digging a hole.

And I've done my best
To fill in the crater
But I always say, "I'll get to it,"
And then I leave it for later.

You see, I've grown thankful
For the darkness inside me.
I'm terrified to lose it,
Fearful of the naivety.

So, I'll continue this path
Of being eaten away,
Because this appetite inside of me
Is the only thing that stays.

Golden Silence

Oh, little one –
You must learn
To think more,
And react less.

Claustrophobic Commitment

Commitment feels claustrophobic –
Like a closed door that I'd much prefer
Was left open.

Options feel like freedom,
And I love space –
Room to spread my wings.

The idea of an eternal routine
Is even more terrifying than death itself.
Because life on autopilot
Isn't really living at all.

Role Models

Your mistakes taught me
A great deal more than
Your lessons ever did.

Rhythm of the Clock's Tick

I'm so ashamed of my actions,
It makes my stomach sick.
Dancing with the thoughts in my head
To the rhythm of the clock's tick.

I can't help but feel this way
When everyone treats me so poorly.
My heart is left in a swollen state,
And everything functions so sorely.

Choke on Your Guilt

Why should I care about
The sorrow that you're puking up,
After all these years?

You broke me down to nothing
And now that so much time has passed,
Why choose to reconcile now?

I can see right through
This selfish mask you've put on
And honestly, I hope you choke
On the guilt that's been eating you up.

My Sweet (Nicotine)

Once I turned my back on you –
The withdrawal was stronger than
Anything I'd ever been a witness to
So, I drew you back into my lungs
With a breath but, the guilt tasted
More putrid than the nicotine itself.

And I wonder why I enjoy you so deeply.
Why I crave your presence.
Why I just can't let you go.

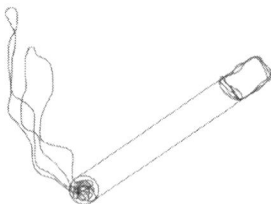

Waiting on the Sun to Rise

Some nights I stay up so long –
Waiting on the Sun to rise and
The birds to sing their daily
Angelic serenades.
But, it seems I spend so much
Time waiting for the Sun
That when she finally shows
Her face, I'm far too exhausted
To even enjoy the view.

The Human Touch

When I was younger, I couldn't wait to leave home. Whether it was to see a friend or go to a party, I was utterly excited about socializing.

Now, it scares me, and I'm terrified to leave home. Some days, it takes hours to convince myself that I'll survive when I step out the door. I despise socializing these days.

I try to study how people do it – watching from afar as they smile and converse, and all with such ease! I regret the fact that I've forgotten how to do it – how to live. There was a time I knew it oh-so-well, but it seems I've lost my human touch.

I Hope You're Not Hurting

I like to watch people doing ordinary things. I like to imagine where they're going; who they're going to see; who they're going home to. I like to ponder if they're happy, sad, stressed, or angry.

But watching people drains me. So, some days I wish I could forget how to empathize because it hurts too much to see such monumental pain and despair. And the worst part is not being able to do a damn thing about any of it.

Now, I'm no saint – even I am selfish at times, but I also hurt sometimes. And because I know how it feels to hurt, I'm unable to wish it upon another human being.

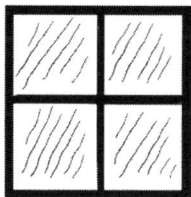

Polished

There will always be
Something better.
Something newer.
Something brighter.
And you can keep hoping
For shinier objects –
As age weighs heavy
On your belongings,
Or you can polish up
The possessions you have
And cherish them for all eternity.

I'm Stronger Than You

All the noise you made
In the back of my head
Will never compare to
The echoes that I will shout
From mountain tops.

I am stronger than
Your need to break me.

The Floodgates

Isn't it magnificent?
That one sound.
One taste.
One minuscule moment
Can open the floodgates
To more than a thousand memories,
A million emotions.

But, that's the price we pay
In order to retain over 50 years
Of knowledge and experience
Into one small collection
Of soft, grey tissue.

Where Does Safety Lie

Where does safety lie
When your home is a warzone?
Where does safety lie
When your mind is such
A danger to your health?
When it continues to test
Your faith;
Your strength;
Your will to live?

Ugly Trauma

Even the most
Ugliest of trauma
Must be dealt with.

Motion Sickness

I find the motion of this world
To be overwhelming,
For it just keeps on spinning –
Even when I can't seem
To catch my breath.

I just wish I could slow things down.

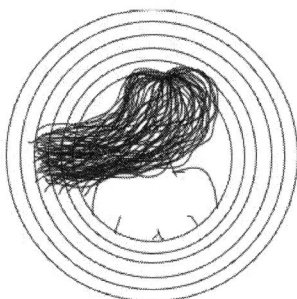

Crack in the Pavement

Sometimes I feel motivated
And determined.
Other days,
I just feel like
Another crack in the pavement –
An object to be walked on
And over, without a second glance.

The Girl Upstairs

I don't like the girl living upstairs.
She's selfish.
She's loud.
She's angry.
My roommate pays no rent,
But uses all my utilities.
She exhausts my wallet each month
As I struggle to keep her satisfied.
To keep her violent emotions at bay.
To keep her insatiable thirst quenched.
But regardless of what I provide
To her endless appetite,
It just won't stop her from
Consuming every inch of my existence.
And I've asked her to move out –
I've pleaded so many times,
But my cries are no match
For her power over me.
She owns this house.

Dead Battery

This life requires endless energy
Of which I cannot provide –
It sucks me dry,
It drains me until I'm like
A dead battery inside.

Occasionally, I can find a spark
Within these water-logged bones,
But the tears have made everything
So damp, after years of aches and moans.

Permission to Fly

The birds do not ask for permission
To fly away with the breeze,
Much like you did not ask for permission
To fly away from my grasp –
All was expected, and yet,
It still brings so much devastation
Watching the scene unfold.

From the Shoulders

The weight on my shoulders
Isn't all that heavy, but my mind
Convinces them that
They're far too weak
To bear the weight
Of all my burdens.

Part Two:

Crack Open My Chest

—

"The fractures on my heart
Create a map of my past
And future battles.

If only I could
crack open my chest,
And lay my heart out
flat on the table."

Nurture Your Nature

You can't grow if you don't take the time
To water your neglected limbs.
We are one with nature –
We too, need to be nurtured
And cared for.

The Missing Piece

I've been told
One, two, ten too many times
That nothing is ever good enough for me,
And they're quite right.
For a moment, I'm happy –
Proud even, and suddenly
I'm contemplating all of the ways
I could be better.
Smarter.
Kinder.
Softer.
Prettier.
And regardless of the effort
That I make towards being satisfied,
I always feel as though there's
A piece of me that's missing.

Hiding from the Sky

One morning,
I looked outside
And to my dismay
I saw the darkest cloud
The sky had ever conceived –
It was right above me.

I waited out the storm
For twenty whole years,
But only realized that
The dark cloud
Just seems to follow me.

One evening,
I looked outside
And to my delight
I saw the brightest star
The sky had ever conceived –
It was right above me.

I hid from the sky
For twenty whole years,
And I missed out
On quite the wonder.

Misplaced Seeds

Who are they to tell you
That you're not beautiful,
Just because you're different?
You are a wildflower stuck
In a garden of roses
And their thorns cut deep,
But you must never conform.

Be you, unapologetically.

Calcium Bones

A bond of calcium molecules
Is all that holds you up,
And you depend on its frail structure
To carry you through this life.
You abuse it,
Break it down,
Whittle it to an unhealthy state –
Unaware that those bones,
Deep in your skin,
Are the only things you have
To help you reach your dreams.
Stop abusing them
And take care of yourself.
Your bones will only heal
A finite number of times.

I'm More Than Just A Body

I am more than my curves,
More than the long hair
That flows down my spine.

I am more than the freckles
Dusted across my cheekbones,
More than just my outsides.

And I hope that someday,
You will see all of me.

Pipe Down

And sometimes,
I love my body so much,
That I can walk with confidence.
Yet other times, I can hardly bear
To look at myself in the mirror.
"Those crooked teeth."
"That lazy eye."
"No one will ever notice you."
This is what she tells me
On my brightest days
And surely, you don't want to know
What she whispers
On the darkest ones –
Comments that could make
Even the toughest of skin crawl.
Some days, I can keep her muzzled
Up enough to love myself
Ever so slightly, and on others -
She's a constant alarm in my head.
Really, I think it's time
That she learns to pipe down.

Flower Brain

This is for the girls
With flowers in their brains –
The ones who only see beauty,
In every ugly face.
The girls that smile,
Even when their hearts
Are in tiny petals,
Scattered across the floor.
This one is for the girls
With fire in their veins
And knives for tongues.

I Hate Me, I Love Me

Sometimes I don't brush my hair for weeks because I just don't care what I look like anymore. I don't remember the last time I took a "selfie," I just can't stand to see my face in pictures. I'm exhausted from trying to impress people who couldn't give the slightest effort in return, and I'm content with despising myself some days so I can learn to appreciate myself more on the others.

Inaccurate Reflections

You are incredible,
Regardless of what
Your mind tells you
When you gaze upon
Your reflection.

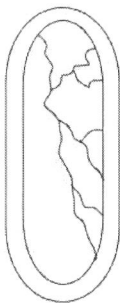

A Wish for the Future

I only wish to be judged
On the contents of my brain,
Rather than the size of my chest
Or the flatness of my belly.

To the Girl I Used to Be

I wish I could have
A conversation with
My younger self.
I wish I could tell her
Not to rage against the world,
But to try and change it.
If only I could hold her tight,
And promise that
Everything will work out.
I wish I could talk to her –
Just for a second,
Because I know how
Stubborn she is
And how she'd listen
To no one else.

Twenty Years to Love Me

I remember having
Big dreams as a little girl,
And somewhere along the way
I stopped reaching for the stars,
The weight of the world pushed
Down hard on my little frame,
And I've been grounded for
Much too long now.
It took almost twenty years
For me to really believe in myself,
For me to finally take an initiative
Towards my life, and I think
I'm almost to the point of satisfaction.
But honestly, I'm okay with learning
Just a little bit more about how
To love myself in a healthy way,
And I only hope it doesn't take you
Nearly half of the time as it did, I.

To the Woman I Admire

If I could be even half of the woman
That my Grandmother is...

I watched her balance
A career.
A family.
A home.
And even some grandkids.

Meanwhile,
I can barely seem to juggle
A simple combination of
School.
Work.
A relationship.
And trying to be a good person.

One day, I will find
The balance of womanhood.

Flower Mouth

I wish I could learn
To have a soft tongue –
A mouth stuffed with flowers.
Instead, I yield a sword
Behind these lips.
Slicing.
Splitting.
Sabotaging –
With every word
That slips out.

Weight for Me

There was a time
Where I felt like
I took up too much space.
And now, I'm worried that
I don't take up enough.
As I fade into the background,
I wonder how I missed the time
When I fit in *just right.*
One day, I'll be comfortable
With the size of my jeans
So, you'll just have to *weight for me.*
But really, I just need to worry
About being healthy and happy.

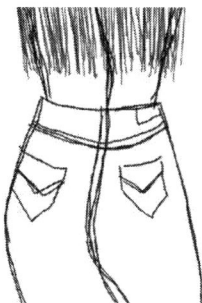

Sex Drive Gone Missing

You shouldn't have to
Feel guilty for
Not being
A sexual,
Sensual
Goddess.
Things get so
Overwhelming,
And you lose your essence.
Be patient with yourself,
Your fire will return.

Capricorn Wars

Being a Capricorn isn't easy.
I'm stubborn as hell,
And so indecisive.
I'm volatile and short-tempered,
Yet sensitive and reserved.
I'm always on the go,
And quick to punish relaxation,
As my mind convinces me
Of all the ways I *haven't*
Accomplished my goals.
I'm empathetic and understanding,
But I can also be so judgemental.
I'm at a constant war between
Accepting who I am
And embracing who
I'm meant to be.

Playing the Fool

I've been convinced that if I can fool
myself, then maybe, I can fool them all, too.
Acting a part is all too easy, until you lose
sight of who you were trying to be in the
first place. And nobody wants to love the
person you're trying to be. They just want
to love the real you; the honest you; the
vulnerable you.

Inanna

There was a goddess named Inanna,
Whom all the land did worship.
Queen of all she ever dreamed –
Not even death could extinguish her.

And she lives on inside of you.

From the Hands

Ten tiny bones ache constantly,
But continue to show up for me
As I dry them out,
Break them down,
Overwork them until
They've cracked and bled –
Continuously making appearances
In the creation of exquisite
And irreplaceable masterpieces.

Women Are Super-Human

You think that you're
As delicate as glass,
When in reality,
You're made of steel.

The Heart Map

The fractures on my heart
Create a map of my past
And future battles.

If only I could crack open my chest,
And lay my heart out flat on the table.

Maybe then, I'd be able
To understand myself.

Alien Brain

All my life
I've felt different –
As if the brain
Dropped in my head
Was meant for an alien.
I love too hard.
I care too much.
I think too often.
I hurt too long.
But, I've come to love
My alien brain.

Violet

Her face told a story
Of a thousand heartbreaks,
As I watched her paint a nude
Cream all over my favourite
Parts of her –
The freckles.
The scar on her upper lip.
The rose in her cheeks.
And she is so beautiful
In every form,
Which is why I cannot
Fathom how someone could
Want to hurt even an inch
Of her delicate, porcelain skin.
As I watch her paint layers
Over the violet marks he left
All over her, I want to crush
The boy's heart in my hands.
But I'm only the best friend,
And I must let the girl
Make her own decisions.

It's Lonely Above the Clouds

You can live atop of your mountain
Built of pride but, you've made sure
That there's only room for one up there.

And it will be a long and lonely life for you.

Crevices

It's not always about
Being on the move –
Sometimes, sitting still
Can help you understand.

Don't force yourself into crevices
That will always be much too small
For your wild, untamed heart.

You'll discover so much about
Yourself if you embrace the messy
Person you that you were meant to be.
You mustn't try so hard at something
That was given to be enjoyed.

So, if the inspiration leaves your
Body, with no post-card telling why –
Trust that you will find a reason
To love the life you live, once more.

Sitting Still

Patience has never been
One to sit with me.
When it comes to the things
I genuinely care about –
Often, I find myself
Unable to rest until
My goals have been completed.
I punish myself for time wasted
During procrastination,
But I've learned that it's more
Than okay to think things through –
Even just for a little while.

The Burden of Wisdom

I've been told that I'm wise beyond my years, and I used to admire that compliment; I used to think it was an important part of me. But now, I'm beginning to realize just how much of a burden it is to be so very mature in this terrifying world.

I've always been just a little bit older than I am, and honestly, I'm trying to be strong enough – intelligent enough – to embrace this gift. But, at the same time, my body aches for its stolen adolescence. I can only hide behind this brick wall made of excuses, for so long.

And sometimes, I wish I could be a little more reckless – be young and stupid while I still can – but, I've made all these plans, and I'm just so much older than I am.

Inspired by Lennon Stella.

Love Like Rain

Loving yourself feels
A little like rain –
Sometimes it soaks through
To your bones
And makes you feel
Oh-so-heavy.

And other times,
It feels like a mist upon
Your swollen goosebumps –
Tantalizing and electrifying
All your senses.

And it doesn't come everyday –
But when it does,
You're thankful
For every drop of it.

Deciding How I Feel

I go through a lifetime of emotions –
Live a thousand lives,
Inside of this tiny brain
Before I reach my destination.

Plastic

I have no desire
For the plastic life
Of which you chase.

I'm content with striving
For experience and intellect –
A purpose within this finite existence.

Brain on the Run

I'm a daydreamer, an imaginative –
My mind can wander so far.
There are holes in my feet
From trying to keep up
With a brain that continues
To outrun me.

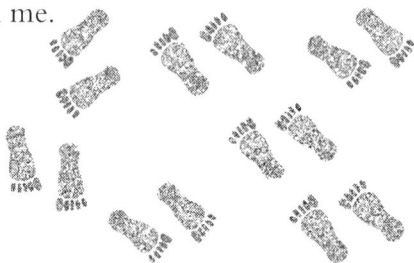

Destined for the Stars

She was destined for greatness
So, the only place she could go
Was
      Up,
          Up,
               And away…

Love Lesson

Learning to love myself
Has been, by far,
The hardest lesson
I've come across –
But it was a good one.

Chemical Reactions

It can be difficult
To rid yourself
Of all the anger
That boils beneath
Your skin –
It feels natural.
It feels safe.

Appetite

I will spoon-feed myself
The love that I so deserve.

The Woman in the Moon

I've heard stories told
To women of every colour
About how the moon controls
So much more than we
Could ever dream.

They say to dance when
Her face is shining,
And to rest
When it grows dark.

We owe it to the woman
In the moon, for all that
She takes care of
On Mother Earth.
From ocean tides,
To the human emotion –
She is queen and goddess
Of all things.

So, why do we continue to cry out
To the "man in the moon,"
When clearly, she is a woman?

A Tough Pill

Satisfaction is a tough pill to swallow,
And I've never been good at
Taking my medicine.

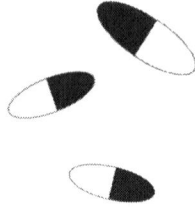

Maleficent Middle

I love beginnings –
The part where you're content
With dreaming of what could be.

And sometimes,
I adore endings –
The part where you've finally
Accomplished all that you planned.

But I despise middles –
The space between everything –
The part where you're forced to
Wait.
Hope.
Contemplate.

Patience has never been
My strong suit.
But someday,
I'll learn to play this game,
And have fun at the same time.

Taste the Regret

Thinking before you speak
Is excellent advice,
But it's useless if you cannot taste
The regret until after the words
Have already left your mouth.

Feminine Intimidation

Strong, beautiful women
Have always left me feeling
Intimidated and defeated,
All at once –
In fear that I will
Never measure up.

Hungry Eyes

Being a girl is a challenge within itself,
And that's before you've added
Seven billion hungry eyes
Onto your adolescent skin.

We must protect our girls
From the beast that lives
Behind all those stares.

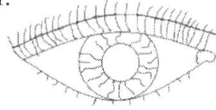

Far from Weak

The heart is portrayed
As fragile, when really,
It's far from weak.

The heart withstands
Great bumps and blows
But still, continues to beat.

The heart withstands
Great trials and hardships
But heals and tries again.

The heart is portrayed
As fragile, yet it bears
The weight of all your pain.

Observations

Take a moment to step out of your skin.
Stand beside yourself, for a while,
And observe one beautiful,
Resilient human being –
The electric and unbreakable bones
Of which you call home.

Make yourself aware
Of the love and dedication
That you owe to your body.

You've Got an Elastic Heart

You're an expert at fitting yourself
Into the tiniest of boxes
And stretching yourself out much too thin,
For all the wrong people.

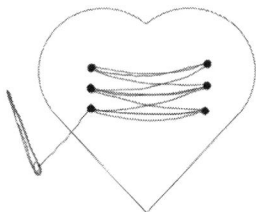

She

She was taught
To work for it,
So that's just
What she'll do.

She paints her nails
As black as the night,
And pins her
Hair up, too.

She makes her way
Through the darkest alleys.
Brushing off every shadow
That dares show.

She belongs to no one
But her destiny,
And the dreams
She carries in tow.

Abstract-ish

I'm not picture-perfect,
I'm barely even abstract.
But, this mess on a canvas
Deserves to be appreciated.

Religious

I've never been religious,
Nor am I against the path.
Honestly, it's just that I don't
Understand such a topic so vast.

I've never been religious,
There are so many things I lack.
But, lately I feel like I could be,
If it meant I could have you back.

Whispers in the Streets

Can you hear them?
The streets whispering,
Saying things like –
"You'll never make it."
"You're too weak."
"You'll be stuck in this town forever."
But, I don't believe them.

I've always known
In the back of my mind
That I would be something
Spectacular.
Extraordinary.
Unique.
Strong.

And I'll be damned
If I let the whispers of this
Boring old town, stop me from
Reaching my full potential.

The Looking Glass

The looking glass is shattered –
The view just isn't the same.
And if I were to point a finger,
Surely, I'd be to blame.

You see, I was exhausted
From seeing things in rose –
Reciting all the clichés,
And learning how to pose.

I needed some inspiration,
From a vision – fresh and new.
So, excuse me while I look through
My newly manufactured view.

One day I may share,
The thoughts behind my ways.
Until then, may you enjoy the scene
Of all the hell I'll raise.

Behind the Cattails

Some days I feel grown –
Withered with time
And wise from all the tales
I've been fortunate enough to witness.
But, then there's the days
Where I wish I could scream
"Be patient with me, I'm just a kid!"
However, I'm twenty now –
Far from my childhood
Hidden behind the cattails.
I made a wish to feel grown
And I've held regrets
For that breath I blew,
Ever since.

Pure Beauty

You are the most beautiful
In your purest form –
Hair tangled down around
Your freckled-stained face,
Naked and free amongst
The moonlit ocean.

It's quite alright if you want
To wear the makeup.
The heels.
The lace.
But, always remember
Just how beautiful you are
Underneath all those layers.

I Will Not Conform

As a little girl I held an ache
To conform with the masses –
Breaking and bending myself
Into the dullest of categories,
Carving out all the pieces
That made me different.
My identity has long felt
Like a mystery to me
But I refuse to continue
To deny all the things
That make me unique.

Love Is Love

You like the way her lips feel
Almost as much as you enjoy his.
All your life you've denied the temptation,
Refused the idea that you could lust
For someone with body parts
Much like yours.

But, darling, nothing about
What you feel is wrong.

What's wrong is
Denying yourself the pleasure
Of being unapologetically you.
So, love whomever you wish to.

Stay True

We're all so ashamed of ourselves –
Terrified to admit how we truly feel,
For fear for inadequacy in front of
Our loved ones.

But, what's the point in all this
If you're living a lie; living in secret?
You mustn't ride this journey for others,
You must ride it for yourself.

So, be whoever you need to be,
Be whomever you want.
But, always remember
To stay true to yourself.

Afraid of the Dark

The Sun begins to bleed
From gold to rouge,
And my mind screams
"I'm running out of time,"
But I fail to realize
That tomorrow is merely
A new beginning.

Little Girl in a Big World

I know words mean nothing
When you're drowning, honey.
So, I'll encourage you everyday,
Until your clouds turn sunny.

Greener Pastures

You must learn to appreciate
This life you've been given –
Do not take anything for granted.

Spend less time on the quest
For greener pastures,
And more time tending to
The wilted grass beneath
Your own feet.

Tenderness

I've never been talented at tenderness –
I feel indifferent towards affection,
And I'm uncertain as to if that will change.

Inside Out

Today was the day I started to feel
Uncomfortable in my own skin.

I thought this was what I wanted –
I thought that I needed to be skinny
To love myself but, I was so wrong.

Because as I picked apart every inch
Of my skin in the mirror today,
I learned the sad truth that the love
I so desperately search for comes from
The inside.

But I've been far too busy
Working on my exterior,
To give a damn about
How my insides feel.

I, Empath

I am exhausted from feeling remorse
For those who have wronged me,
Those who most certainly do not
Deserve my forgiveness.

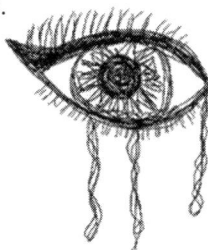

To Be Connected

My knees have buckled
Under the weight of all my issues
And I'm too scared to move them.

There are countless places I'd rather be but,
I can never seem to get my feet there.
There are a million things that I want to
Accomplish, yet everyday I plant myself
Like a skyscraper and wait for the world to
Knock on these shiny doors.

But it never comes, it never knocks,
And I'm beginning to realize that perhaps
It won't ever gaze through my windows –
Certainly not with the curtains closed but,
It's terrifying leaving them agape.

I don't trust what roams beyond
These four walls but, I continue to
Crave it; need it; want it:
To be connected.

The thing I crave the most is also
What I fear deepest – oh, the sweet irony.

Embracing Womanhood

I'm learning how to embrace
My freckles.
My scars.
My acne.
My crooked teeth.
My sexuality.
And even my mistakes.

I'm learning how to embrace
All the things I spent my entire life
Despising, all the qualities
That make me who I am –
Human.

I'm learning how to embrace
All that being a woman entails,
And what I've found is that
It's different for all of us –
There's no right or wrong way.

I'm learning how to embrace
Who I am as a woman,
And today
I'm so proud of her.

Reckless Existence

This year I've been taking it easy –
Being patient with myself but,
Still punishing time spent in
An unproductive state.
As if I don't deserve to be irresponsible.
As if I don't deserve to let loose.
I've practiced being a respectable,
Young woman for far too long
And I plan to enjoy
My reckless existence
For just a little while longer.

Part Three:

Able to Understand

—

"The fractures on my heart
Create a map of my past
And future battles.

If only I could
crack open my chest,
And lay my heart out
flat on the table.

Maybe then, I'd be **able
To understand** myself.''

Finding My Way

I'm terrified to fail,
But perhaps it will be beneficial –
It will teach me something,
And it will only make me
That much more prepared
For the next failure;
The next mistake.

Clarity

Clarity can take some time to develop,
But I'm being patient and trying
To see it all through.

growing...

Appetite

I like to bite off more than I can chew –
Big gulps and heaping spoonful's
Of my deepest desires,
My wildest dreams.

But at the end of the day –
When I fail to complete all that
My list contains,
I still can't help but feel proud.

Success doesn't happen overnight,
However, the steps I took today
Will benefit my journey in the end.
And that's enough to satisfy me.

Chapters

Just breathe.
The struggles you're facing now
Are merely just a single chapter
In your magnificent story.

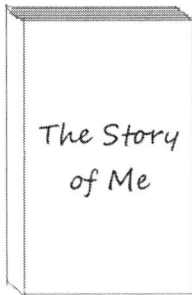

The Story
of Me

The Healing Comes Soon

You can let these feelings tear you open,
Or you can let the pain make you
That much stronger.

Focus on what's important,
And soon enough – you'll find that
The healing is closer than you think.

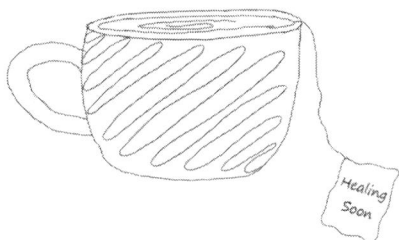

You Need A Trim

Sometimes you're forced to chop away the dead ends if you want to continue to grow in a healthy direction.

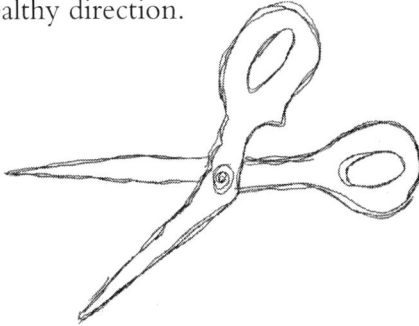

Hazel

Hey, you with the hazel eyes,
Who broke your soul in two?
I see the face you put on so
No one knows what you go through.

Hey, you with the tired smile.
Who told you to be ashamed?
Every ounce of you is perfect,
And you're not always to blame.

Hey, you with the swollen heart,
Who beat you down so low?
I wish you could see yourself in
My eyes, or how you amaze me so.

Hey, you with the hazel eyes.
Did I tell you how beautiful you are?
You've come a long way
And you're going to go so far.

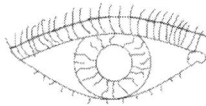

Pretty Faces & Ugly Hearts

A pretty face is nothing,
When you have an ugly heart.
But your enormous one is wrapped up
In gold; and has been from the start.

The strength you hold is endless
And with every step you take –
I know you're bound for greatness.
Believe this, for your own sake.

The Ballet of Life

And though my legs
Are bruised and broken
From running away all the time,
I will learn to dance again.

Getting Your Shine Back

Lately I've been watching the light dance
out of your eyes, and I don't see you
waltzing after it.

I'm no therapist, and sometimes, I don't
even know how to get myself out of bed in
the morning. But when I do, oh, how
proud I am! And you should be, too.

As I watch you pull the hair down from
those sleek braids that you always flaunt, I
wonder where all your confidence went.

You used to shine but, lately you've been in
the gray. So, today is the day we get your
shine back.

Take Me with Salt

Quick to snap.
Quicker to judge.
I'm nothing, if but a fault.

Extremely sensitive,
Vulnerable as hell.
Better to take me with salt.

Always overthinking,
Emotions spewing out.
You're getting close, please halt.

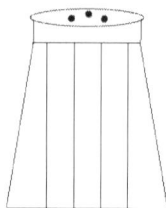

Escaping Your Shadow

My broken heart is mending,
I'm on my way to the top.
You can throw your accusations,
But I will never stop
Until I've reached my destination –
It's so close I can taste it.
I've been given an opportunity
And this time, I won't waste it.
So, I will swallow my pride,
And be the responsible one.
I'm just so tired of living in your
Shadow, it's really not that fun.

Courage Will Pave the Way

I've been learning how to fly,
One fall at a time.
And with every drop
From Cloud Nine,
My wings grow a little stronger.
Redemption is a bumpy road,
But my courage will pave the way.
And the day that I can catch the wind
Beneath my tattered feathers,
Will be the last time
That you ever see me.

Once Upon a Time

One day,
You will be the princess
In someone's fairy tale,
Instead of the villain
In your own story.

Dreaming a Lie

They say that dreaming a lie
Makes the truth hurt even more.
So, wake up before your past
Destroys you completely.

The Waiting Game

I've spent so much time waiting –
For the right time.
The right person.
The right destination.
But it seems through all my waiting,
I forgot to appreciate
What I already had.
And lately, I've been feeling as if
Everything I've been waiting for,
Has already passed me by.

Tiptoe

My whole life
I've feared your reactions –
Tailoring my footsteps
In your favour,
But I refuse to continue
To tiptoe around
Your judgements.

Big Boots Leave
Big Prints on Our Souls

And we're all just trying to be
Better than our parents,
Better than their idea of
A good person.

But it seems as though –
Regardless of how
Hard we work towards
Being more than they ever
Could have dreamed –
We still end up walking
In their footsteps,
They're just so hard
To climb out of.

Slow Down

You must be patient with yourself,
For your body doesn't move
As quick as your mind does.

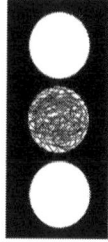

Harmonizing with Sirens

Refrain from justifying your actions
To those around you.

This is your sea to sail,
And if you feel like taking a wrong turn
Just to end up harmonizing with sirens,
Then so be it.

Life is much too short to wonder
Of what could have been.

So, take those risks, conquer those waves,
And never stop believing in your own
Power to keep yourself afloat.

Motive

When do you plan to start
Doing things for *you,*
And *not* for the perception
Of others, and their visions
For whom you're supposed to be?

People are bound to dislike
Something about you –
Something you did.
Something you said.

You'll go absolutely insane
On the quest to please everyone.
So, don't.
Simply do it for you.

The Wind in Your Limbs

I've heard them say
That the wind makes
A tree grow stronger –
That the harsher the gust,
The tougher the limbs will grow.

You can't build up a resistance
To something that you've
Never experienced.

Much like the immune system –
You can't fight off a disease,
Or a virus, that your body
Has never encountered.

All these things take time to learn,
But are essential to your growth.

So, stand tall in the wind, and know
That when the storm becomes
All too much, it's only making you
That much stronger.

Keep Going

It doesn't have to be perfect.
It doesn't even have to be good.
But you must enjoy it,
Or there's really no point at all.

Silent Battles

Some people are just not born
To play the part of strong,
Fearless warriors.

Yet the silent battles they face daily,
Pale in comparison to the ones
You continuously flaunt.

Maybe they can't see you
Throwing punches, but it doesn't mean
That you're not a fighter.

In fact, I think you're quite strong
For not requiring pity, nor recognition,
For your woes.

Organic Happiness

Everyone deserves to be happy –
I mean fiercely,
Genuinely,
Unconditionally happy.

It should never be something
That you're forced to fake,
It should always be
An organic and natural feeling.

If You'd Only Open Up

The things you went through
Are unspeakable, so you make sure
To keep it that way –
For fear of letting someone become
Aware of your weaknesses.

But we all have our demons,
And I promise that you'll feel
Much less alone if you'd only
Open up to someone.

Homeland

The seas are always changing, the waters expand and erase. Waves are pulled back to their homeland and forced upon the horizon again.

The tides rise, and fall. Rain steals and replenishes. And with all the commotion, going on in the oceans, they still find a way to keep pushing on.

Like the sea, you too are always changing. You expand and erase those you love from your path. You're constantly being pulled back to your homeland, only to be forced upon the horizon, once again.

You rise and you fall but, with all the chaos going on in your life, you still find a way to keep pushing on.

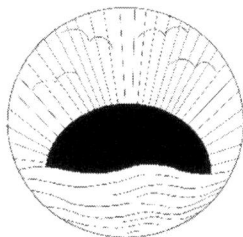

June Jitters

It's not about learning how
To never make a mistake –
They will happen,
It's inevitable.

It's about learning how
To admit that you're human,
But that you'll try better next time.

Our Story

The pages of our story
Have been burnt at the edges,
For they tried to extinguish
The truth we spilled in ink.

The pages of our story
Have been taped back together
More times than I can count,
But our history will
Never be forgotten.

The pages of our story
Have been erased, re-written,
And published for the whole world,
But we will never forget
Who we truly are.

The pages of our story
Have been crumpled, stepped on
And thrown in the trash,
But we will rise again.

Worth the Wait

Don't jump into anything
Child, take some time to think
It all through.
I know you're restless –
Terrified of procrastination,
But if it's something you genuinely
Care for, it will always be
Worth the wait.

It's Okay to Feel

Sometimes, things happen
That will change your life, forever.
And meanwhile, the world outside
Just keeps spinning.

People may stop for a moment to offer
Their condolences, but eventually they'll
Return to their lives and expect you
To do the same.

There's no guide on how to heal,
And there's no right way to cope.
So, cry until you can't,
Sleep until you finally
Feel like waking up,
And rage until
There's nothing left
To be angry about.

You are entitled to your
Unpredictable emotions;
Your volatile personality.
I'm here to tell you
That it's okay to feel.

It's Time for You to Leave

Relinquish these chains
You've tied around me –
My darkest secret –
Let me set you free.
You've been cowering
Inside me for quite some time,
And I think the moment's come
Where we finally draw the line.
I refuse to keep you brewing
And bottled up in here.
So, I'm setting you free,
Regardless of outcomes I fear.

Stay Optimistic

There's no room for doubts
When you have dreams
As big as yours.

Peeling

Gather some strength
And hold your breath.
Your pain is heading
To its final death.

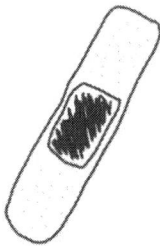

Dig up all the memories
And you may start the healing –
Layer, by layer,
Just start peeling.

Paper Hearts

The day our love
Became a game,
Was the moment I knew
That we needed change.

For, revenge is cold
When accusations are bold
But we can fix all our woes,
So, I've been told.

And our paper hearts
Are good at fall-a-part's
But surely, we can learn
To speak more loving remarks.

Cups

Count the blessings you've been given,
And don't you dare forget
To fill the cups of others –
What you give, is what you get.

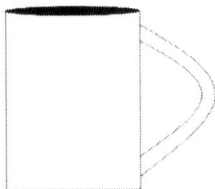

Runaway Youth

My youth is running away from me
And lately, I've been feeling much too old
To even begin to chase after it.

Put the Car in Drive

Just put the car in drive,
And keep on rolling
Until you find a place
Where the streetlights
Make you feel alive –
Where the dark alleys
Hold mystery and wonder,
Instead of misery and trauma.

Just put the car in drive,
And don't stop going
Until you find a place
Where the memories
Are yet to be made,
Instead of the very thing
That keeps you awake at night.

Blossom

Remove the dark clouds
From your existence
And watch yourself
Blossom in the light.

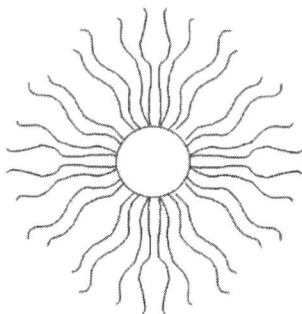

Time

Time is not real –
It's a structure manifested
Within our minds,
One of which,
All humanity chooses
To live by.

Why did we create
Such a confining realm
In which our entire lives
Are constantly defined
By the turning of a hand;
The ticking of a clock?

Time always feels much like the enemy,
But maybe we just need to learn how to
Appreciate and accept it as it comes.

Perhaps time can be a guide
Of which we are merely influenced by,
Rather than enchained and bound to.

Helping Honey

If your emotions hit
Like a tonne of bricks,
Run yourself a warm bath
With a touch of honey,
And let the sweet aqua
Wash all the sadness away.

Lead On

You were not meant
To walk in the shadows
Of your ancestors.
You were born
To lead the way.
So, lead on.

Your Past is Your Power

Rise from the ashes –
Using the flames
As your motivation to push through,
Rather than an excuse for giving in.

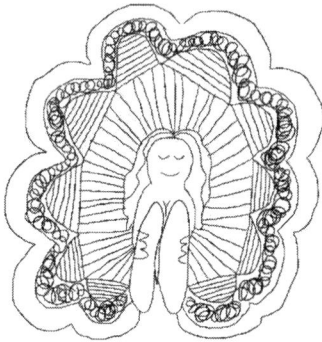

Time to Recharge

Be patient with yourself.

There will be days
Where you feel like
Climbing mountains.
And days where
The walk from your bed
Feels like miles.

You don't have to shine
Your brightest every single day –
That takes an immense amount
Of hard-earned energy –
But you mustn't ever
Let yourself burn out.

So, be patient with yourself,
And know when it's time
For you to recharge.

The Wrong Path

Learn to admit
When you're on
The wrong path –
When the steps only seem
To grow larger than your own legs,
With each passing day.

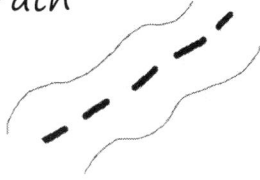

The Light Will Find You

It's been a while since you've felt
The sunshine caress your aching bones,
But I promise that the light
Will find you soon.

I Just Want to Help

I know you're exhausted
From trying to hold it all together.
I wish, with all my heart and soul,
That I could wrap you up in my arms
And let you fall apart,
Because darling,
I will always be there
To put you back together –
Without hesitation.

Stay Soft

Does caring make us weak?
No, I think it makes us stronger.
It's quite easy to be *selfish* but,
Rather hard to be *selfless.*

Peaceful Existence

The bills are overdue,
And you can't make ends meet
When you have no idea where they begin,
But at least you got out of that toxic place.

We all make sacrifices to live a life of peace.
So, remember how far you've come,
How far you will go,
And what you're doing this all for:
Your own peaceful existence.

So, you better damn well
Make the best of it.

You Are Not Defined
By Your Mistakes

We all cause damage –
To hearts.
To heads.
To homes.

Yet our character
Is defined by how
We choose to repair
All the hurt we've caused.

So, choose not to wallow
In your mistakes, but rather,
To seek the knowledge required
For you to fix them.

Gone with the Season

I waited for you,
For as long as I could –
Until the rain pouring down
From the heavens, turned to ivory flakes.
And when I couldn't bear to wait
Another moment longer,
Spring was at my doorstep.
So, I welcomed her in
With the morning breeze
And decided that it was time
To let you go with the season.

Jars of Flowers

I fill every room with jars of flowers
To remind myself that there is immense
Beauty in the smallest, simplest of things;
To remind myself on the days where
I feel less than alive – of what it means to be
A living being on this big hunk of rock.

I, too, am
Plucked,
Cut,
Water-logged,
Suffocated and,
Wilted but, I was also
Damn beautiful in my lifetime.

Good for the Heart, Good for the Soul

I've come to terms with the fact
That maybe you're not always
Going to be the one that I need but,
You'll always be the one that I want.

Chasing A Dream

I'm chasing a dream that moves so much faster than me – continuously a few steps ahead while I choke on the stardust that it leaves in its wake.

Maybe I bit off more than I could chew, or maybe I'm just afraid of what's at the end of the road; scared of all the bumps and curves along the way; scared of the defeat that my choices always seem to walk hand-in hand with.

I am stronger than I give myself credit for, and weaker than I'd like to admit but, I want the change, need the change.

I'm chasing a dream that moves so much faster than me, but I will never stop running.

Billions of Lives

Pride can be difficult when
There's always someone next to you
For comparison –
Someone doing it better;
Someone happier;
Someone richer;
Someone smarter.

Satisfaction only lasts a short while
When there's billions of lives being lived;
Billions of breaths being taken;
Billions of decisions being made.

There will always be a prettier flower
When you're searching the entire garden
And there will always be a taller tree
When you're scouring the whole forest.

You must stop comparing yourself
To the abundances of lives around you.
A life that's better than yours does not exist,
For you'll never be truly happy until
You love the one you live.

A Word of Advice

The best way to face things
Is head-on, with your best foot
Forward, and jammed in the door,
Before they even get the chance
To slam it shut on you.

Diamond

You can bounce all the negativity off you
With your brilliant beams of light,
You just need to stay focused on
What is most important.

Rational Responsibility

You must not try to rationalize with
Your own toxic behaviour.

It doesn't matter what you've been through,
It only matters when you choose to let it
Control your entire existence.
So, don't.

Stop blaming others
For whom you are
Or who you've become.
Take responsibility of your own life.

Counting Lives

Perhaps it's not your accomplishments
That define you.
Perhaps it's the lives you touched,
The lives you changed on your journey –
However short or long it may be.

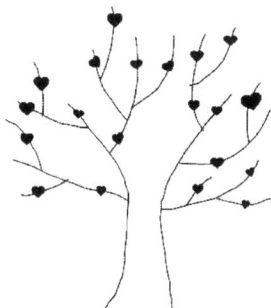

Supernova Heart

You have the heart of a supernova –
The fire burns with such impenetrable heat.

Don't let anyone try to extinguish
The inferno you carry inside.

Upgrading

I have changed more in the past year
That I have in my entire twenty,
And I take comfort in knowing
That the person I am today
Is far from the person I will be
Tomorrow.
A month.
A year from now.

To Give, and Not to Take

I genuinely believe that we amount to what we *contribute* to the world.

But lately, everyone seems so much more concerned with *taking*.

To the Aspiring Writer –

Here's the cold, hard truth: there's 7 billion people in this world and it would be impossible for your words not to hold weight for at least one person.

So, write out your heart, even if you think no one will listen. I'll bet that there's someone out there waiting for your words; waiting for you to speak out; aching to feel as though they're not alone in this difficult battle we call life.

Share your story, even if it hurts. Chances are there's someone out there hurting all the same, and your words could be the rope they need to pull themselves out of the deep end.

If you have words in your heart that you're dying to share, please don't be afraid to let them spill out!

Love, Jenna

About the Author –

Photo By: Matt Lovell
@photomattmedia

Jenna was born in Southern Ontario, Canada. She lives in a small town with her boyfriend and their Siberian Husky. Jenna is currently studying for a bachelor's degree of commerce in accounting.

When she is not writing poetry, Jenna enjoys hiking, reading, painting, photography, being an Aunt, and collecting "Nightmare Before Christmas" merchandise.

The Heart Map is her third book!

You can find more of the author's work on Instagram: @jsbrown_poetry

Other Works –

- **Midnight Memories:**
  A Collection of Poetry & Prose
  (Published: April 2020)

- **Quarantine Dreams:**
  A Collection of Poetry & Prose
  from the Pandemic of 2020
  (Published: May 2020)

Acknowledgements –

I want to start by thanking my wonderful sister, Lisa. From reading the first draft to helping me with the placement of illustrations, all your help did not go unnoticed. Thank you to my loving and supportive boyfriend, Edison. You have always supported my dreams and I wouldn't have half the courage that I do without you by my side. Thank you to my incredible family. All of you helped shape me into the person I am today, and I love you so very much. Thank you to one of my dearest friends, Darci. You never cease to make me laugh when I need it most, nor do you ever fail to be there in my times of need. Thank you to my Uncle, Tim. You inspire me every day. And thank you to everyone who has supported my writing in some way, shape or form. You know who you are, and I'm eternally grateful to have you on this journey with me.

Index –

Manufactured by Amazon.ca
Bolton, ON

17700114R00111